expansions.

micah tasaka

Copyright © 2017 Micah Tasaka
Artwork: Liz Merritt Kong

ISBN: **978-0-9912975-9-7**
Jamii Publishing San Bernardino, CA
www.JamiiPublishing.com

All rights reserved.

Intro/Dedication

This is a year of fire. Burn everything. Burn everyone. To the ground. Start over. Lose what you thought you knew. Pass the threshold. Be born again. Seedlings pushing up through the ground. The changing of the skies. The stillness of the evening. The brightness of the morning. Find constancy in water. Learn to love your ashes. Create a new pattern. Complicate your outlook. And in doing so. Find new ways to be. Abide in love. And in doing so. Be made anew. Heal. Transform. Keep going. As the seasons change. Keep going. Keep growing.

This book is dedicated to anyone who made it through a rough year, those who didn't, and those who continue to keep living. This is for anyone who has ever felt like a falling bomb. This book is for anyone who has watched everything they've built burn to the ground only to find a new way of being at the bottom of the ash, for those who dare to scoop up destruction, pick up the pieces, and start over. This is for the dreamers, the starry-eyed, the resurrected, the burning phoenix expanding her wings to engulf the sun once more. This is for the overly-emotional, the tender hearted, the believers in love who will find their way to truth and speak it out. This is for the healers, those in need of healing, the mystics, the magical sorceresses who blaze their light into an ever-dimming world. This is for you, or whoever can hear me, that you will feel my words, taste my fears, and be opened up to love again and again...

Thank you for taking this journey with me.

expansions.

Table of Contents

Crashing

Winter..5
Explosions..6
Rift..8
Aftermath...11
Event Horizon 5.5.16.......................................13
Down..16

Dreamstate

Spring...21
Upon Returning...22
Oranges..24
Communion Cup..25
Vortex 2.11.16...28
Flying So High. 2.1.16......................................30

Stirring

Half-way..35
Space...36
Reduction..38
There are Other Daffodils...............................40
Summer...42
Alignment..44

Awakening

Meditation..47
Fall..48
Mulch. (a poem in pieces)..............................49
Manifestation...51
When Winter Wakes.......................................56

Acknowledgements...................................... 59
Artist Bios 61

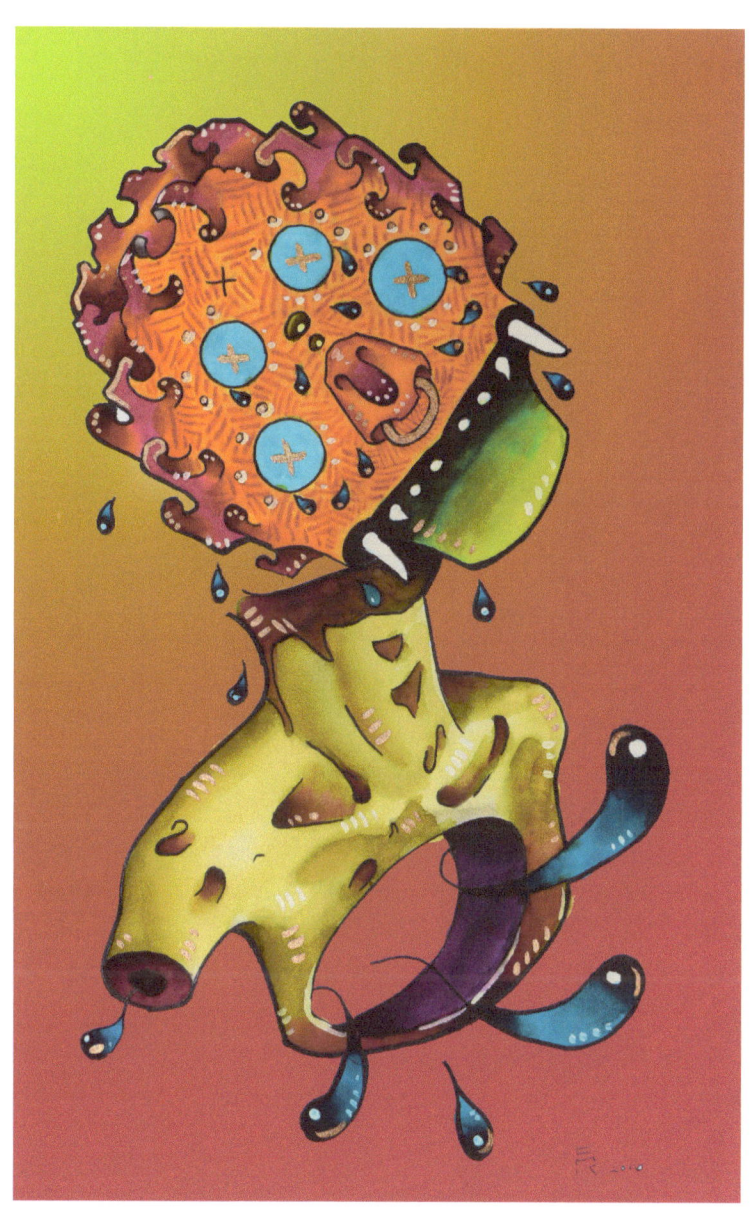

CRASHING

Winter.

And so I began.like a bird swimming in the ocean – ill equipped but still.breathing without gills.Undergoing a careful transformation.reverse metamorphosis into a.truer version of myself.shedding my feathers.adapting my webbed feet for a tailfin.Shrinking in my wings pulling them close until they resemble. flippers. Somehow. I will avoid sinking.Determined to stay alive.I sleep until my lungs grow slits on their sides.Quietly, I teach them to sift through the water to find the oxygen I need. (Closed eye meditation.) I will become much greater than I am now.I will lose my scales.Someday.I will emerge from the water.I will have shed anxieties within me.To the delight of my soul.I will move onward with dignity.My paths directed by the internal voice.trusted with all my heart.Acknowledging the simplest steps as hurdles.I will learn to be patient with myself.Ever so quietly.Crawling before I walk.Mumbling before I talk.Unraveled.loose chord.I will adapt.and change.and love.and survive.

          Mothers and children.
          shed your surprise.
          there is another one
          coming.
          before and after.
          open your eyes.
          either now or later.
          but hope they don't.
          seal shut before next time.
          because then you'll never see.
          We speak in code.
          different languages.
          none above the other.
          striped tongue.
          come undone.
          tell us what you've been holding.
          then relax your jaw.
          and breathe.
          The greatest to abide in.
          is love.
          so dip your hearts under.
          come undone.

Explosions.

My body
    my body
        disenfranchised
            my mind
    two separate jars
      one honey
        one molasses
          both thick
              and uneasily   mixed

      oil
      and
      water
     division
    separation
we will find a way for them to come
                together,
but some of us
    need to be   stirred
      because it doesn't come easily,
and I can only try
        to be engaged
                in the clockwork fruits
                the understanding in each
    …………..carcrash
          there is the
          wrapping
            the tying
            of tongues
      broken in two
      pieces,
s h a t t e r e d p o r c e l a i n

    sometimes I need to be
      baptized in moonlight
          dipped under the sun where
    we can still

    feel the fiery
pulsars
    coming undone
        even now
                      we are unraveling…traveling
the distances

between
us
            with two thumbs
            over each other,
                      can we call this
                      war?
        or
    who are we living for
if we sacrifice ourselves with solid butter
                sep   ara   ting
        in the dish?
I can watch it all go

      down
      but still
find a way
for it to
                stick/to my insides

water becomes wine
    wine in old
    wineskins
                if we find the way
                to still let love in
                before we
    c.r.u.m.b.l.e. and lose our consistency,
honey fruit,

    we will find each other amongst the mess of glass green seas
where some of us some of us will still seek
                      e X p L O s I O n S.

Rift.

      I have sinned
but not against you
                      or against Him
                      I have
    thrust my lips
in between tongues
                          not Hers
                          she
         she once went
      soaring with me
                               departing on solar
                               waves the
              wind beneath me
                  teach me
                                   now
                                what it's like to fall
                   I am I am
                      falling
                                    exhaling
                                    bomb down
                         to the
                  atomic ground
                                       I am
                                       exhaling
                         replaying
                every step and
                                   every purpose
                                     to lose this loss
             and on to the next
                purpose
                             I ache and will
                             once again find myself
          sipping up the pieces
             of foreign glass
                      after the blast
                      where our house
      turned to sticks

                and we went
                                    flying off
                                    into distances deemed
        so far even the
        whales migrate
                                through our rift

                                and if and if

        she comes
        circling back
                        penny
                        train track
we will end
we will end
                            this silly fighting
                            pick out the thorns

preen and relearn
    how to use our
                                arms again
                                and

            if she does not,
                    then
                                I will end
                                my mourning

        with sackcloth and
        ashes dusted into
                                    circles of cloud
                                    we are now
                exiting the future
                leaving the chapels
                                        vacant and colder
                                        than the ice boxes
                        we were born in
                        where our tongues
                                        learned to stiffen
                                        and touch but not
                            crack. We have
                            entered the void
                                            twisting into space

                                                            gravitational pulls
                              ripping us apart
                              and all our attempts
                                                            to not let go
                                                            have only
                              made it harder not
                                to scratch the
                                                            skin beneath
                                                            the surface
                              dermal layer
                              kissed lips blue
                                                      I will remember you
                                                      I will
                  wear your spinning off
                  where I almost lost
                                                      and lost and lost
                                                      into permafrost
                        and froze
               understanding those
                                                those consequences
                                                as a cause
         your magic lantern's
         cost and cast
                                          our nets on
                                          the other side
    instead of trying to hide
                    the sullen
                                                painful truth
                                                that here
                     there are no fish.
                     I wish
                                                it were not true
                                                but understanding
                              me and you
                              this just isn't us
                                                      so we say goodbye
                                                      and learn to cry
                  without ceasing releasing
                     all this to the sky.

Aftermath.

I am elastic
I am elastic
my bones are
made of plastic
that sway through
the blowing trees
suggests to me
that I bounce back

take it in
pieces of the soul
floating in
microscopic
particles bouncing
around in my
now blackened
lungs lingering
like fingertips
to cling
at every piece

but I will
exhale
and after two hundred feet
down in the ocean
I will resurface
and let this go
music of the soul, cry
with the rocks
as no one
sings a single praise
I am emptying my pockets
of the cost
of my being led here
yet again
to feel the aching
in my soul

shatter and reform
I will rebuild
with newer bricks
and open up
my tongue
to drink in the
rain of this atomic blast
filter through
my mushroom lungs
and squeeze out
every useful piece
to water the soil
with the seeds
and watch it all
re-grow
from a different view
certainly
but still it will be
yours.

Event Horizon. 5.5.16.

This day
we shared holy
communion
broke bread
with our hands
dusty as I
protected you from
snakes and you
taught me how to
point out constellations
to find our way
home and
I thought
I'd found galaxies
stretching wider
the confines of
our love
but the truth
is that
even the universe
can be limited
sometimes
by the limits
we place on
ourselves
and now we pick the
thorns from
our hearts
sharing thought
but
distances apart
if only we could remember the
meaning of our laughter
and let it
fill the empty
house with something
but we echo

off the walls
instead
separate our beds
and grow
more icy with time.

If I could explain
the reason we
turned out this way

Do you not think I would?

And now we are
moving
past the boundaries
of safety
made to unlock
ourselves even
deeper than we were
there is another level
and we've surpassed
the knowledge
we once shared
and held sacred
and have therefore
thrown away the book.

There is no sense
in tearing it page
from page,
so why bother?

If I sit long enough
to become still
I will will
myself to continue
growing older as I
must and open up
my soul to trust

that there are
things I don't
understand
so I'm left to wonder
surrendering control
until I am out
of it
and plunging from
the sky
from the perch you took
my up so high
and counting breaths
until
I hit the ground.

I will reach it
and you will know.

Down.

I am the bomb.

          D
             O
               W
                  N.

Watch the ground coming closer as I
        F
         A
          L
           L

Emptying f r a g m e n t e d   destruction
                upon your once quiet life.
      turning you to
      carbon, the
      frail ash
                      Fall.

    I will make a
        mess of things
  splintering even
            the parts you thought were so sturdy.

Keep away
I am atomic
          hashing out
                    sub-atomic
   attempts to love
         I will only destroy you
     and blast upon your
                MUSHROOM clouds
     don't drink
     the rain of
     my aftermath
                  I will stick
               to your lungs and

                        if I don't get you now
in thirty years
                when you thought you were safe
                                            I will appear again
            wrinkle your skin and separate all your limbs.
Unrecognizable and disfigured
                        you will regret
you will regret
            the day I opened up
                                    and
                                    s
                                    h
                                    o
                                    w
                                    e
                                    r
                                    e
                                    d

down
on
you.

DREAMSTATE

Spring.

Abide in love

                at all great cost

even if it stings

                each loss is just

refining to the

                greatest degree

abide in love

                let love abide

in me.

Upon Returning.

Upon returning
so sweet to the soul
closing doors
and creating new
entrances into
this holy land
back when we
used to be sweet,
honey,
accomplished
desire with
eyes closed
made to suffer
no longer.
We
can give up
our guilt and
learn to use our
tongues for
the first time
in communication
to save our
sense of self-
pride with
humility
belief
asked in prayer
received
we will heal
all our cuts
all our bruises
and provide closure
over our
stinging swollen eyes
close and sleep

lose bags,

lady, and
turn your
attention to
yourself
nurture your roots
and let go of
expectation
let love take the
place of
pain and
breathe.

Oranges.

And then there is the love
despite my better programming
that shows up again and again
to teach me
I am not over.

Healing balm
she kisses me
with reverence
for all we both
had to endure
sneaking through
clipped fences
storm the
pearly gates and
ash on the
golden streets

you teach me
there is still more
beyond this there
are still
skies unfolding
and in truth, dear heart,
we can't see the clouds
when we're in them
so keep me on the ground
with your quiet humming
and my shattered parts
burying deep into you
where we can heal
we can heal
we can heal
and come out of this
still
bravely
whole.

Communion Cup.

Teach me to doubt
to lack faith
and then prove it
to me over and over
again in
the breaking of bread
holy communion
the sipping of entire
bottles of wine
sprayed and slurred
through lips drenched
in the blood of christ
that this is what it is
to lose something
silver coin
stolen sheep
to hear the rejoicing
when it comes back
again.

Teach me
to trust in cycles
that we will
rotate and rotate
onward
engulfing the polarity
of each other's magnetism
and spin into gravity
and out again.

Teach me
that love is freedom
love is
watering the seeds
on the windowsill
and cheering

for every sprout
to reach onward
from the dirt
towards the sky
that there will be
celebration
there will be
sorrow
pouring from the
same cup
to open our
abilities to
love and to
ache
that there will be
joy in the church bells
there will be
tears in the
communion cup
but we will still drink,
and we will still
keep showing up
because nothing is sacred
and neither are we
but we do our best
to construct
a religion out of
the smoldering dirt
to offer up new
sacrifice
to better gods
to golden calves
to bodies of oceans
rolling us into our
infinite
souls touch
creating mud and
washing away
impurities

until we are
clean again
dipped into
moonlight
baptized beneath
stars. to claim
our own
as
our own
powerful

we are
powerful
in our love.

Vortex. 2.11.16

This is what
it's like to close
vortexes,
rip bandages,
honey bee,
from our hairy legs
and each time
lose the use
of them and
go on numbing
ourselves with pain.
I will cry for centuries
mourning your loss
heart broken
I will turn inward
become more quiet
become more shy
so that no one will
know a single thought
someday
I will break the
eggshell encasing this
part of myself, but
for now I let it harden
and whisper to
the deeper parts of me
inside the apple seed
the hidden tree
I will grow
past this each
ring rung around my trunk
center of self
I can only age
holding to an
intangible past
hoping for an
undefined future

but forgetting the
present altogether.
A tree without roots
ungrounded
will topple over
and go spilling
its leaves
until it is eaten up
by mushrooms and
beetles to
be reborn
again and again
of stardust
shooting through vortexes
closing and opening

I'll see you again.

Flying so High. 2.1.16

Flying so high

                                              it is easy
                                              to get
                                                                           un-
                                                                           grounded

it happens
all the time.
                        Caught in
                        vortexes/tongues trapped
                                                          freed, open

      we have made it
      to the season
      of love
      and have
      opened ourselves up
      to expect
      the rain to
      come pouring back
      but –
                                    our connection's
                                  still severed.

      Unclaw your hand
        from the couch,
let's divide up
the house, you take
                    what's perfect
                                      and I'll hold the
                                                  rest

tongue of the serpent
mute. flicking feeling sensing,
                      to replace metaphor
                      with meaning
                      just be real to me

                        and we'll learn
                        to speak the same language
                        and bleed the
                        same blood.

As I turn in
my pearls for
rocks and
loose them
amongst the mud

when will differences
blow into wind
when will our
courage come flooding back
                                        as if this is not
                                        the first time I've
                                        broken or the last
                                            I'll, swallow this
                                            lesson
                                            and hope I can
                                            pass
                                    even more gracefully
                                    into the next
beautified with
redundance,
                                recovering from every step
                                taken in vain
                                or lust or
                                un-self-forgiveness
lose it
at once
cast out
two hands
            I tuck it under my tongue
            and listen –

                                                We are our
                                                own healers.

STIRRING

Half Way.

I keep looking
to the sky
to find some sense
of what's
happening
inside of me.
But I am
not that vast
or complex
I just need to be
left
in my solitude
so I can
fall apart silently
here are my arms
my broken wings
all the parts
I have left

        of me
you will fly away
and I will stay
stuck on the ground
upset at my roots
and wishing I could
be there with you
giving up on my legs
I will fall apart
and consider myself
part of the dirt
to lay here
day after day
taking in oxygen
but unable
to complete
anything else
and that's okay.

Space.

Now that you understand
there is no easy answer
breathe through the pain
it is momentary.
Laughter
does not always coincide
with the weavings
of the water's web
but your heart
will still come back.

                                                We were taught
                                                shooter's drills
                                                to vacate before
                                         the bomb was dropped
                                        but some of us are trapped
                                        underneath the weight
                                          of the atomic thought
                                         before the shell hits
                                      sends us all to hell its
                                      not that I believe in
                                      either of the two

                it's just, I think you do, but you don't think you
do. So we squabble our
humble pieces in
squalor planets apart
and rage when we
miss the glimpses of
each other's
blinking lights
from light years across

                                      I used to be able to find you
                                    but now we've grown too old
                                        too quick and I'm not
                                        sure I can recognize
                                            the face I used

                                                            to live within.

                              Space.

Is a medium
I cannot control
as we obey the
laws of gravity
to learn
humility,
we must remember

                                            we are two separate pieces
                                                    fused to one then
                                                            separated,
                                                shattered momentarily
                                                                to be
                                                              rebuilt

                                                               apart.

Reduction.

There are lights
shining
somewhere so full
of planetary posture
bow down, bow down
and make anew
as we scale
brick walls with
our claws like
peacocks
when we fall with grace
unscathed and
able to
put ourselves back on
our feet
somehow
somehow
find the energy
to go on loving
in our solitude
go on
dreaming
in our shadowy night
where we
will become
other versions of
ourselves
compelled
to make the growing
continue on
but tonight
feel free to
crack
if you need to,
drop your eggshells
onto me
I will turn them

into dirt
when my magic
meets your
magic
I will provide the spit
to
create the mud
to set the blind ones
free
and learn to
push miracles
out my hands
and make the rocks
gush forth with
water beneath
them
release your anger
in solitude
release your tears
in the wind
and soon you will
boil down
boil down
to your reduction
stir with honey
and make
yourself sweet.

There are other daffodils.

There are other daffodils
somewhere swaying in
waves swept by wind gusts.
It's not that
these are the last of
the flowers. Feeling
the powers at work
energies meshed and
pulled apart painfully
there is nothing to
gain for me
that cannot be
lost in an instant
Breath. Cold. Silence.
Our lungs turn to tundras, evergreens
flocked with snow
just to let you know
these divisions are
helpful. Just don't
create a border where
there should not be
one but I
will give you time
to recover and rebuild
and I will do the same
celebrating your victories
re-growing past the shame
it took to walk out the door
for the last time
and hang my keys
elsewhere.
There are roots
digging through earth
and plants do indeed
re-grow themselves
but in different soils
with new faces

surrounding older pains
that heal and
with the careful
rubbing of oils
the scar tissue will
dissolve away too.
You have to trust it –
the process of
letting go.

Summer.

And then I began again
poised and ready
to continue plunging down
I've stopped trusting
the ground
beneath me to
be made of anything
at all but
clouds and clouds
trying to be
turned into rain
once we forgive
ourselves of
all our pain
we can easily
let go, fall
into the ocean.
We are only
barely discovering
tapping into the potential
inside our beating chests
sparking the
guiding light
to get us there
we will become
energies of bodies
dancing around
the room so
full of living
we bubble
over
cup runneth
and what I
thought was an
ending was
just the
next page turning

over
cup runneth
to create my
world
so full of joy
in possibilities
I never could have
imagined
to
runneth
cup
over
spill
into
on
around
all
around
like raindrops
flooding the
ocean
like raindrops
stopping short
and then
beginning again

Alignment.

Now that it's summer/leave all the spring behind/and step off the edge/swan diving from/the ledge with/eyes closed and/both arms tied behind./As the lawn turns/brown and all/the trees shrivel up/under this sticky/viscous in the/atmosphere/so heavy upon/so heavy upon/shoulders/under pressure/cracking and/exploding/there's.no.part/of me the sun/will leave in tact./these are complicated ideas/inside the simpleness/of my mind/and I can only swim/towards better oceans/and learn to choose/my battles with/more wisdom/than rage/at the end/ of all of this/the wisdom/that comes/with age/will regress/back to the/childhoods/forgotten the/adolescent/shoved into/teenage closets/and told to/stay silent/there &/wait/I have been waiting/and now see opportunity/to create my world/as I want it./Instead of lingering/in my promises/to you that/I will never leave/in the future, I/will never promise/anything I cannot/and let that be/the tab under the tongue/the lesson sinking/into my spine/musical interludes forever/that I will not/give you all of myself/because some parts/need to be mine./But how will I/survive the heat/ the swell inside/my chest/growing stronger/with every/every wave/edging towards/breaking/and when it does/how will I/keep control/send my body//spiraling through/the air/tossed around   like a child held by/the foot,/baby bathwater,/I will wait for/you to toss me out./I used to feel the power/resting behind my/voice but now/it's broken with/earthquake tremors/and more I/age the/more quiet/I am./I am/quieter than/I always/have been./I will tap in to the source/and remove my/scales my feathers and/learn to walk/in the body/I was born in/this time/proud to live/in this skin/and breathe in these/lungs so deeply/I am becoming/coming into alignment/rising and falling/forgetting/recalling/as all that I've held/resurfaces/and I go, go, go/plunging onward/crazier than I/ever have been/but able/to see/the purpose at/the center of/the cyclone/and/give in to/the wind to/
go flying and/falling/
flying and
falling.

AWAKENING

Meditation.

Wake up.

You are alive,
still floating down
from the clouds,
where energy
and earth collide,
lay your feet
upon the ground.
And keep walking.
Past the burning buildings
past the smoldering
past the water evaporating
then raining back down,
close your mouth,
point your head forward
and keep walking.
away from the cities
away from all the noise and
siren screech,
to where,
you can feel
your
pulse

slowing

and hear

the stillness

in the trees

and breathe.

Fall.

Follow your heart
at all great cost
even when the seeds won't sprout
count each loss
as fertilizer and
continue on
about.

Mulch. (a poem in pieces)

"Hi.
Welcome back to me. I missed you."
Your words now sit in my throat
tugging at my vocal chords until I choke
or am made to breathe lighter
or deeper or higher.

To you,
I will send you fire.
To her,
I will send tears,
and I will rub my face in dirt mounds
blow my breaths into the atmosphere
watch the hawks catch flight
and soar far away from my fingertips
in self-preservation.

In self-preservation
the leaves are shed to the forest floor
to turn the earth
rich. mulch. black.
so new seeds can gain their footing
and push up through the ground
so I empty my pockets
and am found like a rock
dropped into streams
tumbled and rounded
until I am shaped to the piece I am fitted for
and lose everything
that is not solidly a piece of me.

In hopes of becoming a better human
I shed my DNA in exchange for new skins
to slither belly down
on the grassless floor
and with each skinflake dropped
lose the feeling of what they were for.

                                              With each
                                       skinflake dropped
                                       gain the new cells
                   to evolve into whatever creature I am to become:
                                        a tongue of knives
                                 hoping to make it out without
                                          injuring anymore
                                                   without
                                 turning my breath into rocks
                                           I unhinge locks
                                        and let the floods
                                      come rushing forward
                                     welcoming the destruction
                                       welcoming the rebuild
                                because if it were not for wild fires
                                    attuned to the natural cycles
                                       there would not be trees.

                                 So let the winds take the embers
                                  and let the rains put them out
                                         I will find balance here
                                         amongst all the noise
                                       I will find balance beyond
                                            the siren screech
                                          the screaming babies
                              the raging fists still pounding on my car door
                                            the palms opening
                                   the fearful flowers squealing shut
                                      the thunder and the lightning
                                 the voice of god silenced to a whisper
                                           the whimpering women
                                              the dying bees
                                           the hurling volcanoes
                                        the groaning in the earth
                                        because if it were not for
                                            all these tremors,

I would not be the earthquake that I am.

Manifestation.

1. Coming Back Down.

Did we both
have the same dream?
        Where I was with you,
        or was I?
                I'm still waking up
                gaining feeling in
                my body,
                these

are the sensations
of touch
        I reintroduce them
        in spoonfuls
                mixed with sugar
                because I never was
                good at

taking medicine
or releasing it out
        I just
        go inward
                ignore my senses
                live in past tenses
                and float.

But I'm learning
to be different
        reconnecting with the
        moon
                I am becoming
                the ocean
                with each baptism

I am
coming into
fruition
        you are
        watching me blossom

                                                                witnessing what it
                                                                takes to flourish
                                                                without sunlight

leaves grown in
basement colors
                              blue and red, dark room
                              leaking the exposure
                                                                mixing with the fumes
                                                                to catch the perfect
                                                                shot.
I am
skyrocketing.
                              past the limits
                              I once placed on myself
                                                                to never branch
                                                                further than
                                                                you'd go with me
and have therefore
outgrown the tree
                              we used to abide under
                              so of course
                                                                I'd have to find
                                                                a bigger shell
                                                                to live in
instead of just
being comfortable
                              pretending like we
                              always did

                              2. And.

                              listen to the movement
                              it is breathing all around
                                        pulsation
                                        vibration
                                  let those who are lost
                                              be found

        in themselves
                the inmistakable gods
                waiting deep within
where we are more innocent
more quiet
than we remember
but can therefore accept
                all that is
                unfolding
refolding
waving in the wind.
If we
                listen
                and
let it soak into
our skin
may we remember
                we are much older
                much wiser
                than we feel
and if we see our
feet
walking on the ground
                grow roots there and
                remain still
to listen to
the listening of
listeners
                being reborn
                again.

3. Manifestation.

        THIS IS THE NEW AGE:
after the tidal wave
        bomb dropped
    time stopped
        and
  I forgot I knew

                        all the power
            that I am
                        breathing deeply
            in this skin
                        held by
            these bones
                        in contract with
            the earth
                        that I will
adapt myself to learn
                        and then pass on
            pass over
                        be reborn
            and relived
                        so I empty
myself of all my loss
                        and pick up
what is to be gained
                        and when everything is quiet
            I will go inside
                        myself and
            learn to love
                        being there
            instead of trying
                        to escape.
            this is how
                        I want to grow
            I stretch my
                        stock towards
            the new sun
                        and embrace
            the days
                        rounding out
in new moon hollows
                        where I will join you
and you will join me
                        and we will
    resurrect the earth
                        together

                    and shed our
          fears to
                    be placed into new
               skins
                    big enough
for our expansions
                    through time and
     Space. We are
                    expanding
            traveling
                    the distances
          beyond us
                    to
     bring about the
                    new
               to
                    welcome in the new
               to
                    usher in the
                                        New.

when winter wakes.

if I breathe
I will learn to trust the process.
now that winter blows in and
the sunsets against
the smog radiate with
colors more vibrant
than ever before
I will learn to love them
because even on the coldest nights
where my breath turns into fog
the stars somehow
seem to glow even brighter.
As I grow taller
with the trees
and in stillness
ask them to
teach me everything
because I am here
feeling small
in disconnect with the earth
as the systems in place
threaten my very existence
what can I do
but create a world outside of me
like the one I want to see
and shed my fears in the process
trust my own shining light to guide me
into a better conception
of the divinity inside of me
and work to build my communities
instead of raging

in the bull pen.golden calves.determined to set themselves free.might topple down pillars.might crack apart houses.might break hearts in the process.and complain of splinters.drink stale water.and cry over ditches.relieved of thorns.our sides.now ooze.with vines.to trap us in our thinking.where we will wind.the present into our shoulders.but I don't.always have enough shoulders.for all the heads.that want to lean.and still find the strength.to hold my own above my feet.I am doing my best.believe me.but I am still.only human.shedding the.outer dimensional layers.by consuming dry mushrooms.and painting my face with mud.I will lose it in the hills.scream into water tanks.until all silence stops.and I can regurgitate my meaning more clearly.I said.it was all about articulation.but ungrounded so easily.I've learned to float.and never trust my tether.at any moment.but still hope.it can pull me back.to the ground.so my feet.can feel some.stability after.the atomic blasts.blasts us into oblivion.the pieces reassemble.then rise with the sun.to be found.once more.in her fingers.repairing with tape.what sutures used to.suit me, I.release all my expectations.and from an external view.watch it all go down.but still find a way for it to stick.to my insides.water becomes wine.wine in old wineskins.if we find a way to still let love in...

if we find a way to still love.to drag our bodies.once more through this.to prove the outcome all wrong.I would think about it.I would consider it.but I don't know.how many more times.I can afford to be wrong.and you've already spent.all your chances.but here I am.dishing it out.for you.saying.for you.I will leave the doors unlocked.and ignore the clock on my wall.that won't start ticking.in hopes that time has stopped.so I can.get my head together before the next waves.comes crashing down around me.when I'm just trying to breathe.remembering to breathe.trying.to.breathe.and live through this.the momentary cycles out.the dead pulses of our former relatives.made no more than.distant ancestors.relieved of reliving.all pasts converging.into statue-d limbs.will shake hands with the future.and align our children to live past what we could not.our own failures.stamped red on our chests.I will admit my sins.if you just.stop screaming at me.and telling me I'm wrong.for my existence.when I'm only trying to.recover from my upbringing.and take in all the noise.accepting the chaos.with the pain.believing that I am or could be.once again.whole.if I just.become still enough.to stop shaking.and appreciate the freezing cold instead.as the mountains turn purple.and the night welcomes in the frost.I will remember my direction.give up being lost.and find some way.to get my souls.to touch the ground.and contact my purpose here.before moving on to decomposition.and trusting that.for everything there is a process.trusting that.I will make it.through the winter   I will once again
smell the orange blossoms
in the spring.

Special Thanks/Acknowledgements

Thank you to my family: Debbie, Pete, Bethany, and Dani. Thank you to my extended family: Collett Garcia, Liz Kong, Sophie Violette, Mario Sandoval, Samantha Lozon, Sunni Meador for your undying love and endless encouragement and support, I love you dearly. Thank you to Rachelle Cruz for your mentorship and belief in me. Thank you to Angela Penaredondo for your encouragement, feedback, and friendship. Thank you to Vilayphone Tran for holding space with me. Thank you to Traci Kato-Kiriyama, Aaron Weiss, Karineh Mahdessian, Mary Copeland, Joel Lamore, Julie Tilton, Judith Ashton, E.J. Jones, Cati Porter, Lisa Henry, Nalo Hopkinson, Muriel Leung, Vickie Vertiz, Traise Yamamoto, Kamala Puligandla, Melody Stutz, and any other teacher and/or friend who has helped me along my writing journey. Thank you to Jamii Publishing, Nikia Cheney, the PI group in San Bernardino, and all of my spoken word/poetry family (to name a few: Cynthia Young, T.R.U.E, Renato, ferslov, Onna Bailey, Yamina Inzunza, Kacee Kemiah, Aian Mendoza, Juan Delgado, Allyson Jeffredo, Isabel Quintero, Cindy Rinne, and Romaine Washington). Thank you to my RUPO family for listening to me read every one of these poems each week and for providing feedback, applauding, or offering words of encouragement. You've helped shape me, my work, my words. Thank you for helping me complete this project. Thank you to all the queer, trans*, non-binary, gender non-conforming, poc poets of the Inland Empire. Your voice is necessary, keep speaking

Thank you to you for reading this.

Artist Bios

Words/Concept/Layout:

Micah Tasaka is a queer mixed Japanese longwinded poet and spoken word artist from the Inland Empire exploring the intersections of identity, spirituality, gender, sexuality, and recovery from trauma. They received their undergraduate degree in creative writing from the University of California, Riverside. They have performed throughout Southern California and taught creative writing workshops to LGBT youth in the Inland Empire and surrounding areas. Micah's work was published in the In The Words Of Women 2016 International Anthology and Inlandia: A Literary Journey, Volume VI, Issue I, Spring 2016. Their debut chapbook, *Whales in the Watertank*, was self-published in 2014. In 2017, Micah published a handmade chapbook, *Letters to Space* through Inland Empire Publications with the Inlandia Institute group guerillamakesbooks.

www.micahtasaka.com

Illustrations/Cover art:

Liz Merritt Kong is a shimmering Queer/Trans API painter/Illustrator/Printmaker from Riverside California based in Chicago, IL.
Their latest body of work has dealt with the idea of mythology, and the transformation of trauma and survival. Liz holds a BFA from SAIC, is vegan and an avid bike rider.

www.merrkong.com

www.ingramcontent.com/pod-product-compliance
Lightning Source LLC
Chambersburg PA
CBHW041527090426
42736CB00036B/226